THE HALF THAT RUNS

THE HALF THAT RUNS

Poems by Luz Schweig

MOUTHFEEL PRESS

The Half That Runs
Copyright © Luz Schweig, 2026

All rights reserved. No part of this book may be reproduced in print, digital, or recorded without written permission from the publisher or author. Mouthfeel Press is an indie press. We publish poetry, fiction, and nonfiction in English and Spanish by new and established poets and writers.

Cover Design: Cloud Carmona
Interior Design: Kimberly James

ISBN: 978-1-957840-47-5
Library of Congress Control Number: 2025951238
Published in the United States, 2026
First Printing in English $18

CONTENTS

Like Mole Poblano

I
I was born of red sierra clay / 1
The Body Remembers / 2
Fecund / 3
Husks / 4
Thirteen: Homogenization / 5
Summoning Nāhuallis / 6
Memory of Juanita with Filigree Horse Bones / 7
Ontological / 8
Patzcuaro, Autumnal Festival / 9
The Half That Runs / 10

II
Before / 13
Amaranthine / 14
The Flow of Blood / 15
Transplanted, / 16
Huitzilin Heart / 17
After She Left / 18
Disappearing Somnambulist / 19
Unbreakable / 20
Dimming Light / 21
Extinguished / 22
After you died / 24
To Be Freed / 25

III
The Ills of Invasion / 29
Love's Aperture / 31
Conversing with Stars / 32
Drain / 34
The Alchemy of Forgetfulness / 35
Growing Old in the Spring / 36

Elegy to the Desert Wildflowers / 37
Vuelo Perpetuo / 39
Gentrification / 40
Distanciada / 41
Somos Semillas / 42
Confetti / 43
Machete / 44
Verdant Brown / 45
After the Storm / 46

Glossary of Nahuatl Terms / 49
Tlazocamati / 52
About the Author / 55

"I am a descendant of the butterfly people.
Nobody tells us where to go;
we have always known where to go
for thousands and thousands of years."

—Sonia Gutiérrez, *Dreaming with Mariposas*

"See a fence? Jump it."
—Ada Limón, *The Hurting Kind*

I lovingly dedicate this book to
my hardworking Juárenze father,
con todo mi corazón—
Que en paz descanse.

THE HALF THAT RUNS

Like Mole Poblano

If we are light
    then we are light like cuautli:
        ascending past rainclouds
when thunder erupts,
    gliding with life's unpredictable gales
        through soft purples and charcoals,
the same way white copal smoke
cuts paths through the dark temazcal.

If we are dark
    then we are dark like inner cosmos:
        swirling with unexplored depths
decorated with sparks
    of layered identities folded into us
        from the Nahua Nations and Aztlán,
the same way campesinos feed cornfields
with black soot taken from under comales.

If we are mixed
    then we are mixed like mole poblano:
        metamorphed under the grind
breaking out of shells, spilling seeds,
    flavoring what existence pulverizes
        with our ingredients,
the same way barrios in Alta Califas, and
pueblitos in Las Sierra Nevadas share a pulse.

And if we are lost
        then we are lost like buried kernels:
        dormant maize in Tonantzintli's bed,
millions of golden jewels quietly maturing,
        feeding off underground channels,
        preparing to rise, rise, rise
the same way floating Tenocha gardens do
from the cradling embrace of surrounding reeds.

I

I was born of red sierra clay

from Lake Texcoco's womb;
of chilis and hibiscus flowers,
dried and pressed to extract savory juice.

I poured out like blood, wearing
the same scarlet vestments
as the setting sun, the harvest moon.

Born of heritage maize kernels,
radiant like Mars, full of potential: stalks reaching
white clouds, blue skies. My body a five-petaled flor

with circular portals to ancestral wisdom.
Born proud—chest puffed out, yollotl leading the way—
my inner hummingbird sips immortal nectar.

I come from flying arrowheads
red tecpatl stones piercing ignorance
like cacti roots in desert soils.

From the red threads of curanderas
and Mami's pomegranate rebozo, crimson
agave roots shoot into the Earth—

red pozole, ceremonial fires.
Snakes weave pathways into old treasures.
Hawks fantail feathers circling canyons at dusk.

I was born red, like mother's cheeks
when Papi first winked at her. Red
lips, sweet prickly pears.

Like creation, the primordial soup of love.

The Body Remembers

In the city Dad came from,
where he played violin,

my Abuelita nearly died in the fire
that ate her songbirds.

Maybe it was cigarettes,
maybe spontaneous combustion.

We don't talk about those things
that happened in Juárez,

where youth was bought and sold
like trinkets at the border.

But ask my mother and she'll tell you
how Alzheimer's brought it all back.

The body resurrects wounds
before it dies: harkens back to terror

through touch. The brain falters,
after fighting, escaping, crossing,

sweating, surviving. You die again
under an invader's sword.

I prefer fire.

Fecund

The Maguey says she is not going anywhere.
    That she knows me.
        The moment I began to bleed
we converged like tributaries
        carving veins into the desert,
slithering across Turtle Island by moonlight.

These rivers, she says, don't recognize fronteras
    when they curve and shift.
        They rush in to nourish Tenochtitlan,
    to make fluid where this starts and that begins,
        watering ancestral roots,
spreading like a subterranean kalpulli.

The Maguey tells me she's the keeper
    of my bisabuelita's bones.
        Once, all elders sipped
    of her agua-miel, knew the secrets
of her pencas, magically spun cloth
into huipiles from her green flesh.

These stories survive the invasion.
    They slip through
        Meyahuali's skirt of stars.
We weave her flower crown at dawn
    to the sound of suckling—
mouths of newborns gasping for air.

The Maguey doesn't need to tell us
    that she's our mother.
      This we already know.
    She holds us sweet in her womb—
        a spiny quezquemitl, filling pots
with honey for the brown embryos of Anahuak.

Husks

Abuelita tells me I was born in the month of Tlaloc—
part jaguar, part thunder and rain—grown like corn,
in a smoggy valley downstream from the Iztaccihuatl,

where we cooked for the dead: tamales
sweet as suffering. In molcajetes, we mashed hearts
stuffed with the blood of truths omitted while loving.

I don't remember the bullet that split Julio's skull,
but Mother was hypervigilant for the sky to fall.
Death threats, caseloads of Bacardi, comida cold.

Joy coagulates like cars on the periférico, and
we see corruption's fangs taller than any volcanoes.
Negrita is left at the pound. All night camote carts cry.

Then come the trunks, the take-only-what-you-need, leave
the snow on the Ajusco, take Anita Pérez. Feel the bloody
interim between *indigena* and immigrant.

Here, my Anglo classmates pretend I don't exist. When
Abuelita dies, even Tlaloc forgets me in this blurry desert:
Santa Anas in our eyes, on the stingy side of survival.

Some days we even let ourselves feel the grind
of the stone–identity sifting, flattened by the rolling pin.
I want to keep all the husks even when you peel me.

Thirteen: Homogenization

We stopped speaking Spanish
on the other side,

let the new crack our shells,
the California sun sting

raw, turn us into lizards
the same color as cliffs.

We grated our hearts for garnish
on new versions of ourselves,

wore our skins inside out,
felt the acid of migration

burn us like fire and I became
ash—the gringos pecked at my name

like hawks at lizards.

Summoning Nāhuallis

Fear is
a headless chicken
flapping into you at the market,
when you least expect it—
wings tossing up dirt long after
the machete has been wiped clean of blood.

The blade is our phone. It swings
at safety every time the calls arrive
"¡Los vamos a matar!"

In the Plaza de la Conchita some people grab
the rosary, others the gun,
while Mami draws lines in the rug, pacing.

But I was with Juanita making maza. I swear,
she left the virgencita on her gold throne,
summoned the pumas, monkeys and nāhuallis
down from her verdant Oaxacan hills
right into our kitchen in the big city.

She wove protective spells into my black
braids, combed out my anxiety with her
whispery Nahuatl, took me straight to the moon
of her smiling face.

Some will burn copal, others
learn about battle
from the zing-
zing of hummingbirds.

To this day,
though safely tucked into
a California suburb, it's no wonder
Mami refuses to answer her phone.

She didn't have a nursemaid
like my Juanita.

Memory of Juanita with Filigree Horse Bones

When she imagines hooves rumbling down
to the Sabinal river in the summer of 1957,
Juanita pictures the mighty Equus Mexicanus.
She knows the fossils they've left in red river clay,
the same that kept her ancestral skulls. After all,
she's always had the olfactory sense of a quadruped:
has known the scent of wind-swept manes long before
they come into view; how to make tall grasses her bed.
I want to think that somewhere, a moon rises over
those spaces where we are linked beyond morphology.
Now Juanita runs alongside soft chariots only in dreams.
Anahuak's invisible herds, sad phantoms glimpsed
through a slit in the sorbet fog—with downcast eyes,
nearly eclipsed by the advent of genocide—
the history of beheadings, the exodus.

Ontological

I am split earth,
a fissured desert where
once a lake languished.
Now cacti, scorpion
with tail raised, buzzard
overhead orbiting around
what's left. Movements
under my rib cage, an eggshell
ready to hatch little nothings,
ancestral drumming growing fainter
under the Tejano sun, under pressure.
Maybe, you say, we'll make it.
Maybe not. In the meantime, I try
to measure the distance between
whispers and screams, being
and becoming. Sand in my pocket,
destination unknown, I aim my arrows
at the pretty mirage ahead—tierra opens up
to receive them, like the wings of a rebozo
I forgot I wore. Teotl everywhere!
I can't tell where the flapping butterfly wings end
and I begin. The tumbleweeds make music, so much
it makes me cry. Now I see. Here I am.

Patzcuaro, Autumnal Festival

Each year, we listen for their emergence,
the release of what was once encased—
thousand chrysalides ripping open
simultaneously, paper envelopes,
delivering perilous migrant tales.

I know your journey, mariposita.
How caterpillars starve in the waning
tallgrass, how herbicides cough contagion
upon prairies of milkweeds.

It's a milagro we make it through:
sun chasers like them, our flickering selves,
invocations of resilience.

Our antepasados make their reentrance,
and eternity quickens in our hearts.

After the shell breaks, after the struggle,
antennas start twitching in unison.
Indigo slivers of ambrosia, nearing.
We scatter the pollen of resistance.

The Half That Runs

After the last frost melts, winter coats are shed,
coyotes have their pups, and we loosen desert soil
with song—tilling out terror, rooting out the deer in us—
lithic, it freezes before death's speedy headlights.

No one can find us in this canyon. I keep soft sage
leaves in my pocket. *When afraid, inhale.*

Papi says the shifting course of the Río Grande
cut us in half, so we landed on both sides of the Chamizal:
One part was thrown into a basket; the other runs
like a halved chicken after the butcher's chop.

We are the half that runs. Each spring, we follow
the blood stains of those that ran before us.

Mami says a mountain lioness came to inspect
our work one morning, make sure we still knew
how to dance like eagles, listen to the land
weave baskets from willow leaves, be still.

I don't know the road off Black Mountain.
But I know where the biggest cacti grow, how to move
like a tumbleweed, light a fire with sticks and stones—
dry grasses from the sunny side of the hill. Patience.

No one can find us in this canyon. Sometimes, though,
I think I see the light moving closer. Don't freeze.
Light sage. Take a deep breath. Run!

II

Before

The year Dad lost his job,
harpoons flung in our direction.

I wore kelp capes, swam west
to the edge of the earth,
learned buoyancy alongside seals
until my skin grew barnacles,
marine mists swallowed me.

Here was better than there, so,
in Alta Califas, I befriended papaya-colored
garibaldis, circled the legs of wooden piers,
swept sandbars alongside nurse sharks—
rip currents in my chromosomes.

It didn't matter that the sharp spears
of hunters aimed for our slippery scales.

Some of us take longer to crawl onto land.
We flop like a fish on sand one year,
sprout primitive appendages the next,
like baby Cipactli.
There are no directions for such a recipe—
It mixes where it wants to, resists where it doesn't.

In water, everything is remade.

It's said Tangaxoán's daughter, the Purépecha princess,
—is now the mermaid of Lake Zirahuen:
vilified like the rest of us for her tails, her voluptuous breasts,
her sorcery and serpentine braids dark as star-nets.

As a half-this, half-that,
I found myself returning to the sea,
to remake myself—in magic,
in turquoise, in the lexicon of quiet.

Before "them" before "us."

Amaranthine

I remember milk souring in the fridge,
overripe guavas in the fruit bowl,
noisy flies orbiting around the unsaid.
Where I come from, stories burrow
in guts and marrow instead
of trickling out of mouths.

Downhill from the pepper tree,
we kept our truths sealed up tightly,
like marmalade jars expiring on shelves.
When we hurt, we talked about
Santa Anas blowing in from Anza Borrego,
conejos on the hill, refilling the dog's water bowl—

This is how we encoded heartaches
in the ordinary, kept moving forward,
barricaded our feelings for fear
that we might disintegrate.
Yes, mi familia buried things for progress:
painful histories, fears, even secret daughters.

We became listless voices inside vicissitudes
of migration—ears deaf to the urgent pecking of
words trapped inside eggshells. And to
this muted story, bound for the compost with
bruised guavas, the stench of unspoken aches
filled the house like dead bodies do graves.

The Flow of Blood

We harvest volcanic rock
this side of El Xitle
for Mami's garden:
carry ashen, porous clumps
through Tlalpan's woods.
Whose bones do they hold?
How long have they soaked
in the hot sun?

In the nopal field, once
we found a shriveled
umbilical cord, hint
of an infant, womb, life
bursting forth at its own pace.

I smelled rain in the distance,
heard Dad's guitar in the wind.
Mi hermanito giggled as he slid
down a dry river bed, his joy a hawk
carving circles in the sky.

We followed the trail out of the navel,
thunder drumming around wet
lava-rocks turning black as hair
in our hands, adornments
for cilantro beds, manzanilla,
homesickness.

These are the things we take with us
when we hemorrhage north.

Our cords snap,
as we wander wet
into life after the womb. . . .
El Xitle doesn't object,
though I wish he had.

Transplanted,

our kitchen lime tree grew wildly:
leaves proliferating, limbs lengthening,
defying my previous procrastination
to find the right size pot, dig gingerly around
the periphery, lift her out—keeping all roots intact.
That spring she grew luxuriant and free, offered
fruits fragrant with yesterday's joy, filled our cups
after we'd been shoveled into shock, hurriedly
chopped at the base, stems mishandled, told to
pass for white while withering—lest all our leaves
drop off. But they didn't, because we took turns
sipping of her limonada, swirling life's pulp gently
on our tongues, as we slowly rooted into new soils.

Huitzilin Heart

Remarkably, we still usher in spring
        after invasion and bloodshed,
after homes are abandoned, helter-skelter.
        We confer between hills,
learn to expunge life from cacti,
        hover over thorns, oceans away.
Forget the long-plumed eagles,
        and their high-flying summer sun.
Our transcendence is in wintering.
        We fly low to the earth,
hang upside down like bats,
        sing of Huitzilopochtli.
The human heart is an inky cavern,
        a scratched record replaying
familiar exodus songs as chambers empty,
        like cities, era after era,
the left ventricle receives, the right contracts,
        spilling out refuges, all aflutter,
zooming in, ruby-throated, zooming out, violet:
        the clear sky opening up ahead.
Here, we share maps to escape routes,
        learn how to let go,
decorate the stratosphere with the hum
of wings—tomorrow, we'll build new nests,
        populate them with eggs,
let life enter us again, in tiny sips.

After She Left

When I walked in Leti's room,
hollowed out like a pumpkin,

after she ran away—that night
of unending dog barks and

coyote howls—sitting on the bed
in the dark, was our father. And

he startled me, at first, because
he didn't look like himself: head

hung, broad shoulders hunched,
glasses resting on a nearby

nightstand. But there he was
gently stroking Leti's white cat

with one hand, while wiping his
dark, Indio eyes with another,

the hallway's bright light glistening
off his wet face. I'd never seen

Papi cry like that before: whimpering
in pain, like a tiny rabbit stuck

in an unforgiving trap. No matter
what I'd heard of Rosarito beach,

or him leaving us for another woman,
I knew we were his only real home—

Resting my hand on his back, it both
soothed and terrified me: the way

Dad's lungs gasped for air,
the way my own breath suddenly stopped.

Disappearing Somnambulist

Scientists say around 200 plant and animal
species vanish daily. That we'll never again

hear the songs of the slender-billed grackle
of Toluca, swim with the charco azul pupfish.

Mami says our exotic creature is Leti—tall
like a giraffe, hair that crackles with sparks

when she sleepwalks: 1,000 fireflies trapped
in a net. Not born of a womb, but of baby

axolotl clouds, pink donuts, the look on a dog
that's been invited on a walk with no leash.

Museums keep the long plumes of grackles
on display, the way Mami keeps our Leti's

guitar: dusty and alongside the phantom
limbs of her cantos, the memory of Papi's

claps, his ¡*Otra, otra!* Maybe, if we had
known how to leave wild things alone,

we'd be able to bring Leti back, magically
refill our woods with the beautiful, the extinct.

Unbreakable

Papi makes me a kite
    from purple tissue paper,
        with his elegant fingers

on Mami's kitchen table.
    He holds onto the sticks
        as I brush on glue:

underneath too, he says. *Así,*
    so the wind won't break it.
        Neighbors see me run

down to the vacant lot
    at the end of our street.
        I am all kite, feet, smiles.

I don't remember the sky
    swallowing my kite that day.
        Just the sound of the paper

flapping, Changuita barking,
    mis amigas cheering, *you're lucky*
        your Papi makes kites!

Today, on the way to the post office,
    I pass a vacant lot,
        picture one of Papi's kites

in the hands of another little daughter:
    before me, before Mami.
        The little girl is smiling;

she glued her kite just right,
    she knows the sound
        tissue paper makes

    when the wind lifts it—¡así mero!
        Her tight stomach thinks
            the paper will rip, but it doesn't.

Dimming Light

Dear Father,
In your world of books and brine,
among urchins and octopi, you swam,
whale-like, having forsaken desert dust,

breaching infinity with curiosity. Your

brain, more voluminous than any encyclopedia,
netting bedtime stories for me, like minnows
splashing in my mind, keeping me awake

with excitement for *elsewhere*. Not this

smoggy city on a school night, but mermaids
under Sirius singing me to sleep. I remember
us sailing the seven seas, unearthing sunken

treasures glistening in the sun—your eyes

tiny stars lit up by my nightlight, your hands
bats flickering with each word. And, much later,
I remember your winter years spent in the room

with the giant T.V. clicker in hand, lighthouse

lost behind a gauzy fog of forgetfulness,
and I too late to board, having miscalculated
how gluttonous the sea is for sun.

Extinguished
Driving up the volcano

Whenever it snowed on the Ajusco
we vacated the city to forget.

In a smog-line, wove our way
out of the broken valley, and up

toward the cumulus peaks.
It was how we buried things,

how we pretended nothing hurt:
packed the car with tortas,

sarapes, secrets, and yielded to
hibernal amnesia. It wasn't something

we had to do. Rather, it was where
the cold sent us each year after

Huitzilopochtli's birth, when
sun hovered low to the earth,

a hummingbird. That's when
Mami sipped enough of Papi's mentiras

to mistake them for truth-nectar, and
earthquakes hinted at subterranean lava

bubbling out of the cracks in their marriage.
Mistakes can happen in an instant,

but the secrets they spill out are long,
like ascending carreteras.

I grew feathers on those rides,
learned to fill in the cracks with wet clay,

move with the river currents, watch
smoke dance as it rises. So,

when Papi took his last breath,
many snows later, exhaling

fifty-year-old secrets
I already knew how to match

the breath of the volcán,
whisper my way through pines,

roll down pastures like morning fog,
into the twinkling metropolis below:

just a little glimmer in the distance
against the dark advent of our escape,

hissing embers giving rise to the
opaque smoke that was my father.

After you died

I wished for your spirit to fill the room
like a gauzy fog bandaging ether around me.

Waited for the lamp to turn on and off again,
by itself; a meteor zenith before dawn.

Your flannel shirt: epidermis; your untuned
guitar: La Malagueña dusty in the corner.

That year I baked you pan de muertos
until anise and orange swarmed the house,

fed fire to more candles and copal than
the Cenzontle has songs, the nopal thorns.

A professor once told me that *religare*
is Latin for "to reconnect," as if you were

a god, and I was clawing up the oak tree
in our backyard, hoping to pounce on the moon.

To Be Freed

From the cliff, an old man on the beach
worked slowly to free a young seagull from
a tangled net, removing his glasses, gently cutting
through nylon, while wings sliced light
streams every time they flapped, sun flickering
on and off, low in the sky, peeking through pier legs,
over sudsy foam, the sound of the winter tide rising,
whooshing back and forth, the horizon darkening.
The man, now holding the gull to his chest, still
fiddling with feathers and net, sitting on dry sand,
is moving his mouth, maybe as he delivers
comforting words or even a song. I strain to hear
in the salty gale now whipping against me and
my own wish to be so tenderly freed.

III

The Ills of Invasion

When it rains, it rains stories.

On my rooftop, we barrio kids gather
to hear Conchita tell of the Noche Triste,
in 1520, when Spanish swords
      waited, waited, waited

for the sound of joyous drumming:
(our ancestral drumming), before
      slicing-off the arms
and legs of the danzantes.

They timed the massacres perfectly,
for when we were happiest.
Dogs stop barking to listen,
and gray lizards freeze on pink walls.

Here in Tenochtitlan, we have two seasons:
the rainy season when we thrive,
and the dry season when we wither.

In me, also, are two seasons:
the writing season, when I dance;
the dry season, when I get sick.

The doctor says the drought
is in my *Latina DNA*.
Nahua DNA, I correct—
25 million slaughtered
ancestors in my genes.

When the withering starts
they spill into my veins all at once:
ancient danzantes with phantom limbs—
feet stomping, ankles rattling,
reawakening my Earth with ayoyotes.

With copalli, together
we try to smoke out the topography
of terror, drum life back in,
revive the medicina of the earth.

Lightning flashes before healing,
as the huehuetls and I reprogram
the rain-dance back into me.
Flushing genocide out of my cells.
One mazehualiztli at a time.

Love's Aperture

Lulling calls of owls between tree branches
        eclipsed by strands of pings jolting my arm
toward the nightstand, where my phone records
        orgullo, delivered in rapid-fire succession.
Mami types fast and furious on the opposite
        coast in her Saltillo tile home: of how fever
took Dad's father when he was just a boy, how
        he swept and mopped floors to help feed his
little sister, aunt, mother, and *still was first*
        in the family to finish eighth grade,
first to make it across, send half his salary south,
        pay for abuelita's cataract removal,
save us from the sepia lens that was Juárez.
        I just want people to know, appears on
the tiny screen aglow in my palm: love's aperture
        heavy in my chest, as I text back through
darkness, *I'll make sure they do, Mami.*
        Ping, ping, ping—No sleep again tonight.

Conversing with Stars

Yesterday, I learned
   that space recycles stars—
      That when one burns out,

     it splashes out sparks
   of elements that birth new stars;
they travel in clusters like fish.

Maybe, if I look long enough

into May's night sky,
   I might catch a glimpse
     of Papi, swimming in space,

     25 million light-years away:
   his giant fins causing constellations
to sparkle with each sweep.

Papi died in the spring
   in the brown reclining chair,
     without morphine,

     before sunrise,
   as elliptical galaxies
emerged from cosmic caves,

like whales from deep sea.

I empty my heart into Ursa Major tonight.

Every cell in me
   wants the trio of time,
     dementia, and distance

THE HALF THAT RUNS

    to return him to me
   so that we may contemplate
the minutia of our ebbing existence,

the edge of the universe,
   and what's beyond the beyond,
     as we once did when I was a girl.

Drain

The year floods broke the drought senility unspooled father's secrets,
strolled with them under blossoming cherry branches, delivered them

as if asking for a second serving of quesadillas and guacamole, until
their frequency became synonymous with mother's clenched jaw.

Some days are better than others, even for denial virtuosos. Today, she
holds the shell of their 50-year marriage on her lap like a piñata that bled

bats instead of candies when it broke open. This wretched season flaunts
petal sundresses at her, dusting them with pollen gold as the bouquets Papi

gave her when he came home late. Of course, Mami sees a mistress in every
cherry tree—dignity in every ax. We pry his boxed ashes from her wrinkly

hands, brush her gray tresses, offer her mango licuados, chop cilantro for la
comida. Which way to the 13 nahua heavens, now that we live north of the

Gila River? We dust, open windows, perfume the ether with magnolias and
lantanas to mask the moldy words mushrooming in the basement of the unsaid

as Mami pictures father's soul spilling like flood waters into the Zócalo,
sinking the cathedral with its weight, looking for a drain to flow into.

When the dismembered cherry tree litters the driveway the next day,
we say nothing. We notice Mami's wedding gown pours out of the trashcan,

like a silk waterfall. She stands by the window in anticipation. Who cares if the
flood-waters drain into Mictlan now? The garbage truck has come and gone.

We slice papayas and lemons, refresh vases, bring conchitas from the panadería,
and, best of all, Mami sings again. Hard-working hands resting softly on her lap.

The Alchemy of Forgetfulness

Mother inhabits
memory caves.

Like a bat,
she follows sound waves:

phantom melodies
of my father—now ash,

playing guitar,
singing her love songs,

barely reaching her
across death and darkness

and wings of anger, flapping.
How many lies has he left us?

I would like to
take her out to the garden,

where springtime
spills violet flowers,

where hearts lighten.
And bury him again, there,

under the jacaranda tree he planted,
before the alchemy of forgetfulness,

with the sun caressing us—
muting the cave, at last.

Growing Old in the Spring

After lunch, Mami steps out onto the patio,
pulls up her plastic chair, faces the hills.
The rabbit she fed earlier returns for more.
Mami wobbles to a stand, notices her slippers
are still on, slides the door open, heads back inside.
When she steps out again ten minutes later,
she brings carrots, wears cheap chanclas.
A red-tailed hawk circles overhead—
Hide! Mom warns the rabbit. A neighbor hears,
the dogs on the hill bark, the rabbit's brown fur
blends in with California desert, the hawk flies on.
I come out just in time to hear Mami sigh.
She offers me a tired smile, proudly points to
her own little patch of desert glowing with gold
acacia blossoms. *I water every day, just like
your father did!* Pulling up another plastic
chair, I sit beside her, pour our agua de Jamaica.
The silence between us is as soft as her hand.
It shrinks, like my Mami. It holds the energy
of wintering, despite the flowering hill,
the wet earth, the offerings of fresh carrots—
reminding me that the hawk is still hungry.

Elegy to the Desert Wildflowers

It's fire season.
Mami is prepared with full gas tank,
family photos in a box by the front door
for easy evacuation.

She holds us in her box,
as we float on boats in Xochimilco,
mount horses in Chapultepec,
rim the same table, flowers filling our vases,
cinnamon bites of arroz con leche on our tongues.

In Mami's box, gordito giggles on my lap.
She takes a wooden brush to Leti's hair:
long Apache silk down to waist,
her famously long cuentos spicing ether.

Best times of my life, Mami says.
When I had all my babies near.

Now we're all scattered:
run disoriented with the grass rabbits,
and black-tailed deer.
Our feathers singed, like those of
California quails, sad sparrows.

We've stood under ashen rains
of 100,000 acres of trust,
blazed through in one fell swoop.
Smelled non-native cheatgrass-infernos
char inland montes of honesty overnight.

Nothing can measure the speed of pain.
Who could ever imagine that invasive grass
feeds off car exhaust? That the aimless
let's-get-somewhere-fast is kindling
for flames to jump from shrubs, to cacti,

to Joshua trees in the heat of the moment.
Rush hour traffic stealing oaks
from savannas, like children from mothers.
All seedlings scorched.

I know because it's been over twenty years
since the rosy buckwheat buds grew here—
the violet sage, manzanita. Two decades
without the blue-winged swallowtail butterfly, or
giggles around our kitchen table over birthday cake.

But it's fire season again.
And Mami's evacuation box too small
to fit the bobcat, the gray fox—
all the desert wildflowers.

Love turns ashen here on Black Mountain.
The exhausted firefighters collapse,
our table vases empty.
And we, unable to see the lit match
still burning in our hands.

Vuelo Perpetuo

Lloro ante los cerros, hechos cenizas,
trigo polvorizado, culebras quemadas.

Lloro ante la ausencia de mi padre, y humo
que asciende de manera triunfante, final.

Aquí entierro los cuentos de corazones
mudos y sin orillas como la descuidada tierra,

o esta soledad que sostengo en horas disfrazadas
de sombras y luz, lagartijas desprendiendo piel.

Siento que eternidad se asoma como un sol
parpadeando y yo encima de su pecho.

Ay, qué día tan silencioso, y a la vez salpicado
con los llantos de mi madrecita envejecida.

Hay cuervos confundidos que vuelan de una
espina ardiente a otra, sin donde aterrizar.

Gentrification

Tell the man watering his lawn in khaki shorts on Lamont Street:
once, the whole universe imploded on his green turf;

a chasm opened up and swallowed the light, death's ferryman
made a collection, the contents of a bleeding womb were spilled.

Tell his wife—home early from Pilates, planting tulips under the trellis—
to dig tenderly around the banana tree, around the hijita-that-never was,

now less than six feet deep, sans gravestone, in secret: dust-to-dust.
Maybe mention that she buries her pricy bulbs atop love's remains:

the fragile skeleton of what-could-have-been, of joy.
A mourning mother cries in the car parked across the street

holding ropes that prevent the ferry from leaving the shore: her hands
as raw and red as her eyes, her pickled heart canned in grief,

one contraction at a time. This was years ago. Before the divorce,
the for-sale-sign, the stranger in khaki shorts, the baby. Lost.

Distanciada

Mami shuffles her pantunflas as she paces
back and forth on her beige kitchen tiles—
Come have your panecito, Mami
I say each madrugada before birdsong
and her reminiscing: all on Leticia
and how she won that book-reading contest
in elementary school, taught herself Italian
overnight, was the más lista of her babies.

Let's go visit Leti! Mami asks me,
several times a day, with hopeful eyes.
And—over and over—I don't know how to
explain the fights, the silent treatment,
the estrangement—that Leti hasn't wished
to see us for years. Instead, I make Mami
otro cafecito, watch her crack open a bolillo,
pull its bready softness out, dip it in her coffee,
pop it in her mouth with a girlish smile.

After sunrise, Mami sits in the patio near
flowering hibiscus, counting red-breasted
hummingbirds. She's kicked her pantunflas
off and is warming her feet on the concrete,
wiggling her toes. Out the kitchen window I
watch dementia continue to crack her open,
pull her softness out, dip her in innocence, give
her happy tunes to hum—because she thinks her
Leti will be joining us for la comida, because
grief inhabits us in unexpected ways, because
in the end, it seems love triumphs over anger.

Somos Semillas

After Papi died, Mami wilted fast,
let her yard brown, hair whiten, skin
grow delicate like moth wings.

Neighbors say she stopped sweeping,
waited each twilight with her cafecito,
for Xolotl to rise over the vecindario.

She waited for her ribs to collapse,
her heart to grow lengthy tendrils
into the earth that swallowed him.

We all came as fast as we could
after the forty flower offerings,
after the cancer and canciones,

cooked her favorite dishes,
hovered over picture albums,
took turns with the guitar.

Pero she had already rooted herself
in his Indio bones, nothing left now
but brown earth, dry yard, seeds.

Confetti

In the city of your nativity,
in the house five blocks south
of Mercado Reforma, past the paletero
with the wobbly cart.
In the exodus out of
Guanajuato's silver mine bowels,
where Tata's lungs collapsed to invasion.
In the residue of Carlota's Castilian butchers,
bloodstains from the Pueblo revolt.
In the sudden shift of the Rio Grande
and the dirt courtyard where Pipo lived—
best rooster in all of Juárez—a short
walk from Bar Azteca where gringo
soldiers preyed on you as a boy. In the
imported cattle they raised for bullfights,
Tonantzin streaked with border lines.
In your mother's empty pantry,
tsunamis in your stomach, sharing half
a tortilla with your little sister. In the sound
of you whistling rancheras, up early, spraying
the pavement in front of our home. In
the jail en la esquina de Calle Ignacio
Mariscal y Avenida 16 de Septiembre,
where you first worked as janitor, big dreams
brewing in your head. And in that other desert
where your firstborn daughter now lives,
observing monarchs migrate across highways:
So many, she texts me, *they become
confetti when I drive into them.*
In the place where saguaros graze
stars, (in all those places, and more), that vast
terra incognita between who you were
and who I am. In what moves at such fierce speed
it outruns your ghost—orange paper wings
scatter everywhere, almost festively.

Machete

After ballots were counted,
    morning came like an imperious eclipse
glutton for light, forcing águilas to their perches.

This is when Juanita would say
    that we are also the obsidian butterfly,
seeing without sun, deftly navigating darkness.

Juanita hasn't heard of election results.
    Instead, she listens for wind
whipping her milpa into pollination.

January twentieth is not on her horario.
    But she knows to harvest her nopalera
when the moon is full, flavors ripest.

In sexto grado, I was the flag bearer,
    marched proudly in the escolta, singing:
¡Guerra, guerra! los patrios pendones
    en las olas de sangre empapad.

So when I picture myself with Juanita
    harvesting cactus for tacos,
it's all I can do not to swing her machete
    like a macuahuitl at the dark.

Verdant Brown

As autumn's broom sweeps the green away,
a moth's butterfly-like wings remind me
that somewhere, spring is happening, unseen,
languishing under the epidermis of race.

Meanwhile we suffer post invasion,
dig for remnants of ourselves in the compost,
reintroduce seeds of former selves
in this sectioned, labeled, unyielding terrain.

I used to spend long nights listening for the
watery return of Chalchiuhtlique—that we'd yield
more of us next harvest, adhere to the law of the corn,
bring seven snakes to cultivate our fields.

Now I resonate more with the skeptical earth—
hands blistered from tilling myself out of the dry clay.
How long before the hills wear jade skirts again?
This machete has dulled from chopping new pathways.

Still, I try not to trip on protruding roots: each one
electric with the suggestion of hope, worming into the
depths of me, defying impermanence. Together we
thirst for frog-chirping rain, wait for ashy clouds.

Can you hear the white-water rivers shapeshifting
over dams, soaking inherited milpas? Can you hear
us, genocide's progeny, using our metates again?
Verdant with cricket songs: brown earth finally drinks.

After the Storm

When the thunder stops,
  I will listen for the sound
of galaxies blowing out of conch shells:
  Ehekatl swirling through
my inner and outer space.

  I will become a tiny grain
of sand, slipping through
  colonialism's sieve,
free-falling into eternal Aztlán.

  At first, I'll be a wet newborn,
struggling just to breathe—
  Meztli watching,
ambiently, from the summer sky.

  Later, I'll become
a silvery river, flowing under
  millions of sparkling eyes,
celestial black hair.

I will learn to exhume
stars from night's dark soil,
  sprinkle them like
condiments over lingering aches.

  I will learn acceptance,
unfurl fists into open palms
  like pink perennials,
use a sharp tecpatl blade

  on my heart, tossing
the innocuous into compost:
  Nourishing harvest ahead.
At last, the antecedent
  to loving the darkest dirt.

GLOSSARY OF NAHUATL TERMS

Ajusco	Volcano located just south of Mexico City, which I could see from our home. Originally named Axochco, or "flowering place from which water flows"
Anahuak	Nahuatl for "close to water," the valley of Mexico
Aztlán	Ancestral home of the Mexica people—both literal and metaphorical
Cempazuchitl	Mexican marigold flower used in Día de Los Muertos rituals to beckon deceased loved-ones with its fragrance
Chalchiuhtlique	Ancient Mexica feminine maternal concept symbolizing fresh water rivers, streams, lakes and fluidity in life
Chamizal	Stolen ancestral lands between present-day El Paso, Texas, U.S.A, and Ciudad Juárez, Chihuahua, Mexico
Chapultepec	Meaning "on the grasshopper hill" in Nahuatl. Now, the largest urban park in Mexico City
Cipactli	First animal to crawl onto land from primordial soup, according to ancient Tenochca culture. The name of my childhood school.
Copalli	Copal incense used in specific ceremonial and healing rituals
Cuautli	Eagle concept representing bravery, the sun, warriors
Ehekatl	Essence of wind—the carrier of seeds, songs, and words
Huehuetls	Wise elders and sacred drums in Mexica culture
Huitzilin	Hummingbird symbol of light, warriors and resilience
Huitzilopochtli	"Hummingbird on the left side," or our heart: the inner sun

Iztaccihuatl	Volcano in Mexico City, Nahuatl for "white woman," referring to the snow-capped peaks of the volcanic range depicting a reclining woman's ette, which I'd pass on the way to school
Kalpulli	Cluster of homes, barrio, community
Lake Texcoco	Site of the ancient city of Tenochtitlan, now Mexico City's center
Law of the Corn	Mexica paradigm that views corn as sacred, stating that that each crop grows stronger than the one before it
Mayahual	Ancient Nahua Maguey goddess representing the mother
Metates	Grinding stones used in Mexico since antiquity for grains, vegetables, etc.
Meztli	The Moon, symbolizing the womb, fertility, the emotions.
Mictlan	Complex concept of the afterlife in Nahua culture
Milpas	Sophisticated ancient polyculture farming system unique to Mesoamerica that created a self-sustaining ecosystem
Molcajetes	Mexica mortar and pestle traditionally made of volcanic stone
Nāhuallis	Sorcerers, shapeshifters, animal spirits
Nahuatl	A group of closely related Uto-Aztecan languages spoken in central and southern Mexico, and Central America
Noche Triste	The "Sad Night" when Spanish invaders slaughtered of all dancers of Mexico-Tenochtitlan sparking a bloody battle on July 1 of 1510
Periférico	Name of main interstate in Mexico City
Purépecha	Indigenous people centered in the Northwest region of Michoacán, Mexico: one of the few empires that defeated the Aztecs
Quezquemitl	Indigenous-made shawl worn since pre-Hispanic times

Tangaxoán	Last emperor of the Purepecha people
Tecpatl	Flint stone made of quartz, often decorated with symbolic drawings to indicate calendrical themes. The quintessential original tool
Temazcal	Ceremonial clay hut representing the womb
Teotl	Life's sacred energy
Texcoco	Main lake in the ancient Anahuac, of Valley of Mexico
Tlaloc	That which the Earth drinks, like the rain
Tlalpan	Partly forested area of Mexico City
Tlazocamati	Expression of deep gratitude form the heart
Tonantzin	Mother Earth, Nahua concept for the Mother of all life (Tonantzin Tlalli Coatlicue)
Tonatihu	One of the words for 'Sun' in Nahuatl
Xitle (El)	Volcano in Mexico City, from the Nahuatl Xicyli, meaning navel
Xóchitl	Flower in Nahuatl, the last day (20th) of the Tonalamatl, or Nahua calendar
Xolotl	Nahuatl for Venus as the evening star
Yollotl	"Heart" in the Nahuatl language
Zócalo	Originally, the center of Mexica civilization, where a teocalli, or sacred pyramid, once stood. Now, the main public square in Mexico City

TLAZOCAMATI

Many thanks to the editors of the following fine publications, who first featured earlier versions of some of the poems in this volume, originally published under a literary pseudonym:

Scott Russell Duncan-Fernandez and Jenny Irizary, former editors at *Somos en escrito: The Latino Literary Online Magazine*, for being the first to offer encouraging critiques of these poems. And, together with Armando B. Rendón, to publish the first poems from it in January 2021.

Odilia Galván Rodríguez of *Cloud Women's Quarterly Journal*, Dr. Raina J. León and Lupe Méndez of *The Acentos Review*, Jarred White of *Penumbra*.

Katie Lynn Johnston of *Mulberry Literary*, for choosing my poems as the first-place recipient of the inaugural Mulberry Literary Fresh Voices Award, and to Carlos Fidel Espinoza of *Barrio Panther Literature Magazine* for your encouraging critique.

Elizabeth Jiménez Montelongo of La Raíz Magazine, Natalie Crick at *Fragmented Voices*, the editors *at Visual Verse*, Siobhan McKenna—for her very thoughtful editorial suggestions—and *Yellow Arrow Vignette* for nominating my poetry for "Best of the Net."

Dr. Vicky Bañales, founder and editor of the social justice literary arts magazine *Xinachtili—Journal X*, for including my work in her inspiring project.

Brenda Vaca, founder of Riot of Roses Publishing House, for publishing my *Somos Xicanas* anthology (December 2024) in which one of these poems appeared.

Adrian Ernesto Cepeda and Edward Vidaurre for including one of my poems in *Anger is a Gift: Poetry Anthology of Resistance and Response Poems to the 2024 Election* (Flowersong Press, 2025).

It was an extra special honor to have this manuscript selected by former U.S. Poet Laureate, Juan Felipe Herrera, as one of two runners-up for the 2024 Andrés Montoya Poetry Prize.

Many thanks to Luisa A. Igloria, the 20th Poet Laureate of Virginia, for her invaluable guidance. Y a mi querida amiga, Carolyn Chilton Casas, for giving my manuscript her proofreading magic.

Mil gracias to my publisher, Maria Miranda Maloney, who persuaded me to relinquish the literary pseudonym under which these poems were originally penned, and claim my own voice.

I am especially grateful to Graham, my love, for always believing in my voice and helping it land on these pages, even—at times—through playful and somewhat annoying dares.

Finalmente, un agradecimiento especial a usted, querida Maestra Hilda, por ser la primera en publicar uno de mis poemas titulado "Primavera" en la revista literaria anual de mi escuela primaria.

ABOUT THE AUTHOR

Luz Schweig (she/her/ella) is a Xicana poet raised in Mexico-Tenochtitlan and Southern California. Since 2012 her contributions have focused on anthologizing marginalized voices, especially those of women. Her latest anthology, *Somos Xicanas* (Riot of Roses, 2024), is a historical contribution that illuminates the enduring legacy and evolving presence of Xicana identity and culture through the voices of over eighty Xicanas. It received the Dolores Huerta Best Cultural and Community Themed Book, along with the Best Women's Issues Book Awards at the 2025 International Latino Book Awards.

Luz's own poetry—previously published under a pen name—is a first-place recipient of the Mulberry Literary Fresh Voices Award, and a Best of Net and Pushcart Prize nominee. Her first poetry manuscript, *The Half That Runs* was selected by Juan Felipe Herrera as one of two runners-up for the 2024 Andrés Montoya Poetry Prize. Luz is a former editor at Somos en escrito Literary Foundation, and a board member of MeXicanos 2070. She defies conventional educational norms and stigmas as a self-taught writer whose eclectic work aims to participate in community building, challenging stereotypes, resisting settler colonialism and reviving Indigenous eco-spirituality.

A proud Abuelita of three, Luz lives by the Powhatan River on occupied Tsenacommacah territory with her beloved life partner and her dear elderly mother for whom she acts as caregiver.

www.ingramcontent.com/pod-product-compliance
Lightning Source LLC
LaVergne TN
LVHW090038080526
838202LV00046B/3867